More
Aussie
Bible

More Aussie Bible

Re-told by Kel Richards

Bible Society NSW

More Aussie Bible
by Kel Richards

Published by Bible Society NSW
5 Byfield Street
Macquarie Park, 2113
NSW

May, 2006

Text:
© Bible Society NSW

Illustrations:
© Graham Wade. Used by permission

Layout and graphic design:
www.madebydesign.com.au

ISBN: 0 647 50917 2
Printed in Australia   2006

www.theaussiebible.com.au

Contents

The story of the Aussie Bible

It all began, believe it or not, with an English school teacher named Mike Coles. He was working in the East End of London, where he found that most of his pupils didn't have a clue what many Bible passages are about. So he began re-telling some of the stories of the Bible in the street language of the East End—Cockney rhyming slang.

The result was published as a book called *The Bible in Cockney (Well, bits of it anyway)*. When I came across this little book I was delighted by the Cockney lingo—and also struck by the fact that Aussie is a distinctive branch of English every bit as colourful as Cockney. This thought inspired me to do for Aussies what Mike Coles had done for Cockneys. The result was *The Aussie Bible (Well, bits of it anyway!)*.

This was published by Bible Society NSW in 2003 and went on to sell well over 100,000 copies. Since then I have been encouraged by the number of people who have told me that this little book has inspired them to go back to reading the Bible again (a proper translation of the Bible, that is) or who said they were inspired to start reading the Bible for the first time. And every time they told me this they asked for more bits of the Bible to be re-told in Aussie English.

In fulfilling their repeated requests, I should explain that there are four types of translations (or paraphrases)—some of which sit really tightly to the original text of the Bible (the Old Testament in Hebrew and Aramaic and the New Testament in Greek), and some of which sit much more loosely to that text. Listed from the tightest to the loosest they are:

Word-for-word translation
Thought-for-thought translation
Paraphrase
Re-telling

The Aussie Bible belongs in that fourth category. In other words, this is Bible storytelling—admittedly it's Bible storytelling that aims to stick to the original pretty much sentence-by-sentence, but it's still storytelling, rather than translating or paraphrasing.

In the first section (From Genesis) I aim to re-tell the beginning of the Bible's account of God's intervention in human history—hoping that you'll be inspired to take up the Bible and continue reading the story for yourself.

In the second section (From Proverbs) the goal has been to put some of the Bible's little gems of poetry and wisdom into Aussie English.

In the next section (From John's Gospel) I turn once again to the main message of the Bible—which is all about Jesus Christ: who he is and why he came (including chapters 20 and 21 of *John's Gospel* re-printed from *The Aussie Bible, (Well bits of it anyway!)* to make the story complete).

Finally, I have re-told the whole of John's first letter in Aussie—with its great message of love as the key to life, the universe and everything.

The Bible really is God's message to humanity—and here's a bit more of it in the bewdy, bottler language of Aussies.

Rip into it—you'll find it's as bright as a box of budgies!

Kel Richards

From Genesis

In God's workshop *(Genesis 1:1-27)*

Out of the blue God knocked up the whole bang lot. It emerged as a dark lump and God ran his mind over the swirling surface.

The universe was Voice Activated: God said, "Let's have some light!" and bingo—light appeared.

"Looks good!" said God, as he drew a line between light and darkness—labelling them day and night. This bit began and ended: Day One.

God said: "Let's have the H2O where it's needed," and it spread and divided into clouds and oceans. "Heavenly!" said God. That bit began and ended: Day Two.

God said: "Let's have rivers, lakes and oceans, with good farmland in between." It happened, and God labelled them land and sea. "Excellent!" said God.

God said: "Let's have plants, flowers, vegetables and all kinds of fruit trees that'll grow from seeds." It happened: plants, flowers, vegetables and all kinds of fruit trees growing from seeds. God was pleased. That bit began and ended: Day Three.

God said: "Let's have the stars and planets sorted out, marking day and night and the seasons of the year, and giving light and warmth to Planet Earth." It happened. God had the day-time dominated by the sun and the night-time by the moon (and God also fine-tuned the stars). With day and night, sun and moon taken care of God was well pleased. That bit began and ended: Day Four.

God said: "Let's have the waters and the air full of life." The result was a swarm of different kinds of fish and birds. God said: "Good onya! Now, breed up—and fill the place!" That bit began and ended: Day Five.

God said: "Let's fill the Earth with animals and insects—breeding and growing all over the planet, from big four-footed beasts down to slithering reptiles." And God was pleased to see the planet bursting with life.

God said: "Let's make *homo sapiens* representing Us and resembling Us." So he did: *homo sapiens*, male and female, representing God, resembling God, and made by God.

Running off the rails (Genesis 3:1-24)

There was this really snaky Enemy (morals lower than a snake's belly and cunning as a con-man). And he said to the sheila, "Did God actually tell you to grab your lunch off any tree in the garden?"

The sheila replied, "You got that wrong. Our fruit salad can come from the rest of the orchard but strictly off the menu is that one tree in the middle.

God says if we even touch that we're dead meat."

Then that snake-in-the-grass said, "You won't die! God knows as soon as you eat that you'll see what's what, unplug yourself from him, and start making up your own rules about what's Right and Wrong—you'll be your own god."

The sheila took a good squiz at the tree in question: it *looked* good, and she thought it might *taste* good, and she wanted to see what's what, so she had a bite, and she passed it on to her bloke, and he had a bite too.

At that moment they saw what they'd done and felt exposed—starkers. So they knocked themselves up some clothes out of leaves and things. When they heard the sound of God heading in their direction the two of them, husband and wife, hid in the mallee scrub.

"It's pointless hiding," called God. "Come on out!"

"I heard you coming," said the bloke, "and I hid in the scrub because I was starkers."

"Who told you that you were starkers? You've been at the tree, haven't you? The one I told you not to touch?"

"Don't blame me," said the bloke. "It's that sheila you gave me—she put me up to it."

Then God said to the sheila, "What have you done?"

"Don't blame me," said the sheila, "that sneaky, snaky one lied to me—pulled the wool right over me eyes."

Then God turned to the Enemy and said, "You're really in trouble. You're as full of poison as a taipan, and you're the lowest of the low. You're dirt, that's what you are. It's open warfare now between you and the woman and her offspring. In the decisive battle you'll attack her Offspring's foot, but he'll beat your brains out."

To the sheila God said:

"From now on your labour pains will be terrific, and no matter what you want from your husband he'll call the shots."

To the bloke God said:

"Because you let your wife tell you what to do (when I said not to eat from that tree) from now on the ground itself will be your enemy, growing weeds, thorns and thistles: farm work will be an absolute curse—tears, toil and sweat just to grow enough wheat for bread. And in the end you'll die, be buried, and turn into worm food."

Now the bloke was called "Adam" (or "Man") and he called his wife "Eve" (or "Life") because she was the mum of everyone who lives.

Then God made some proper leather clothes for the two.

God said, "These *homo sapiens* have turned themselves into Law Makers (just like Us) making up their own rules about what's Right and Wrong, so it'd be dangerous to leave them within reach of the tree of everlasting life."

So God drove them out of the garden, into the wilderness to the east, and put a guard on the garden so they couldn't get back to the tree of everlasting life.

Edifice complex (Genesis 11:1-9)

At the time the whole human race spoke the same lingo (and no one ever had to learn irregular verbs).

As the population drifted east they found a saltbush plain in the Shinar district.

There they put their heads together and said, "We need building materials, and bricks would be just the shot—given there's not enough stone around the place."

"And with our bricks," they added, "let's build a great city—a mighty metropolis—and let's whack up a dirty great tower, reaching up to the clouds. It'll be a monument to *us*! We'll be famous! And the city'll keep us together, so people don't start drifting away."

And God saw what they were up to: the city, the tower, the whole towering ego thing. God said, "When they scheme together like this it's only the beginning of what they'll get up to. They'll stop at nothing, this lot. Let's go and break them up into different language groups so they can't scheme together. Let them babble at each other."

That was the end of the big building scheme, and people drifted off across the whole planet.

That's why the place is called "babble"—because that's where God put a damper on their arrogance by giving them heaps of different lingos and scattering them around the world.

Abram hits the wallaby track (Genesis 12:1-9)

Now God said to Abram, "Time to pack your swag—leave the old homestead, your dad's place, and all your rels. I'll show you where to go. I'll make you the founding father of a great mob of people. You'll be famous. You'll be a real blessing. I'll look after everyone who looks up to you, but I'll write off those people who write you off. Through you flows a blessing for every type of person on the planet."

So Abram (later called "Abraham") did what God told him to do.

He was already an old codger of 75 when he nicked off from the family homestead at Haran. He took with him his wife Sarai (later called "Sarah"), his nephew Lot, wagon-loads of stuff, and the usual bunch of camel handlers, rouseabouts and hangers-on.

They set out for, and eventually reached, Canaan district.

They travelled as far as Shechem and the big oak tree at Moreh. (At the time a bunch of savage pagans called Canaanites were living there.)

God spoke to Abram and said: "Your offspring will one day make their homes here."

Then Abram moved on to the high country up above Bethel where he pitched camp (with Bethel to the west and Ai to the east). At that campsite Abram built an altar and prayed to God.

Then they all packed up and moved on, in the direction of the gibber desert of the Negev.

How Joseph ended up in Egypt *(Genesis 37:1-36)*

Jacob (a descendent of Abraham) lived as a drover, moving his herds and his people around the Long Paddock in the Canaan district.

This is what happened to his family.

Jacob's son Joseph was a 17-year-old stockman working the sheep with his brothers, and he used to go back to his old man and dob his brothers in, which he got away with because he was the favourite—the apple of his dad's eye (because Joe was born when Jacob was an old bloke).

Jacob (who was also called "Israel") got this really lairy coat for Joe—lots of colours and no taste.

The result was that Joe's brothers couldn't stand the sight of him—they could barely bring themselves to speak to him. To make matters worse he told them about a dream he had. He said: "In my dream we were all baling hay in the paddock, and my bale stood up straight and all your bales bowed down to mine."

His brothers said, "So, you reckon you're gonna be the boss cocky, do ya? Reckon you'll end up giving us orders?" They were really teed off (because of his dreams and what he said.)

Then he had another dream. "This time," Joseph told his brothers, "the sun, the moon and eleven stars were all bowing down to me!"

He told this one to his dad as well as his brothers and his dad ticked him off, "What rubbish! Do you reckon that me and your mum and the rest of family will end up bowing down to you? Get a grip, son!"

His brothers were dead jealous, but his dad kept puzzling over the whole thing.

One day when his brothers had driven the sheep

over to some better feed in the Shechem district Jacob said to Joseph, "I want you to go to your brothers over Shechem way."

"No worries," said Joseph.

"Report back to me," Jacob said, "on how the sheep are doing, and how your brothers are keeping."

So Joseph took the track from Hebron down to Shechem.

He saw a swaggie on the track who said, "What are you looking for, son?"

"For my brothers. Have you seen them or their big mob of sheep?"

"Yeah, I saw them. I think I heard them say they were going to try to find some pasture around Dothan."

And that's where Joe found his brothers – in the Dothan district.

While he was still some way off they saw him on the track and said, "Look out fellas! Here comes The Dreamer!" And they planned to knock him off.

"We could kill him, throw him down a gully, and say that a croc attacked him, or something. What'll his dreams amount to then, eh?"

But one of the brothers, Reuben, said, "No—we shouldn't kill him. I don't want his blood on my hands. But we could throw him down a steep gully that he couldn't 'ave got out of, and leave him there." (Reuben was actually planning to rescue Joe, and get him back home to his dad.)

When Joe arrived his brothers tore off his lairy

coat and threw him down the gully. It was a dry gully with no water at the bottom.

Then they put the billy on to boil and sat down to lunch around the campfire. They looked up from lunch and saw a travelling band of Ishmaelites (also called Midianites) approaching, their camels loaded down with perfumes and the like to sell in Egypt.

Then Judah said to the other brothers, "There's no money to be made by just killing Joe. So, let's sell him to these blokes as a slave. And that way we won't have his blood on our hands—after all, he's a pain in the neck but he's still our brother."

So they pulled Joe out of the gully and sold him for twenty bucks to the Midianites who were passing on the track and who took him off to Egypt with them.

Then Reuben came back to the gully and found Joe gone, so he went to where the rest of his brothers were camped and said, "The kid's gone! What am I gonna do now?"

Then they had a bright idea: they took Joe's lairy coat, killed one of their animals and dipped the coat in the animal's blood, and sent the blood stained coat back to their old dad with a message saying, "We found this. Do you reckon it's Joe's coat?"

Jacob, of course, recognised it at once: "It's my favourite son's coat! He's been killed! Some wild animal's got him! Maybe... a dingo got my boy!"

And Jacob just couldn't stop crying. He sobbed for days and days. His other sons and his daughters tried to comfort their old man, but Jacob just sobbed, "I'll go to my grave with a broken heart."

Meanwhile, down in Egypt, the Midianites sold Joseph as a slave to a bloke named Potiphar—a captain in Pharaoh's personal bodyguard.

From Proverbs

The key to common sense *(Proverbs 9:10)*

Being smart *starts* with having respect for God! Unless you have some idea of how great and good God is you haven't got a chance of knowing what's really going on!

Wise words from smart old Solomon *(Proverbs 10:1-10)*

Having a sensible son makes the old man dead pleased, but a dill of a son will bring his mum to an early grave just from worrying!

A lying rip-off merchant scores nothing in the end, but doing what God has in mind delivers a bloke from death.

Do what God wants and you won't starve, but go in the opposite direction and you're headed for nothing but frustration, sport!

Bludgers end up without a brass razoo, but elbow grease pays off in folding money.

When it's time to run the combine harvester over the paddock that's when it's smart to roll up your sleeves and work hard; only a real goose would nod off in the shade!

You'll be okay if you stick to God's path, but a bad bloke's mouth brings him nothing but trouble.

People are happy to remember a decent bloke, but they just want to forget a bloke who's a slime-ball.

If you've got an ounce of sense you'll listen and learn, but a drongo will just rabbit on and on and end up learning nothing and knowing nothing.

Stick to the straight and narrow and you'll be okay, sport; but if you start twisting and scheming people will tumble to you sooner or later!

If you turn a blind eye to what you shouldn't; and if you're all mouth and no action you'll end up stony broke.

Stay on track (Proverbs 12:1-20)

You wanna end up smart? Then learn to love being set right when you're wrong; but if you hate being told "You got that wrong!" you'll stay dumb.

God wants you to be a good bloke, but if you get all devious and snaky God will write you off.

Bad blokes are always on shaky ground; but a bloke who aims at doing the right thing is as solid as a tree with deep roots.

A good wife is a bloke's pride and joy; the opposite is like having a bone-deep disease!

A good bloke even watches what he *thinks*; but a bad bloke will always be scheming how to stab you in the back.

Bad blokes use words to trip you and trap you;

but honest words can be a real life saver.

Bad blokes end up falling in a heap; while good blokes stand their ground.

Everyone respects common sense; but no one likes warped thinking.

Better to be a humble hard worker than a celebrity with a towering ego but nothing for lunch!

Good blokes will look after their dogs and livestock; but bad blokes couldn't give a toss.

If you wanna eat—then work hard; only a dill loafs away the day!

The greedy want everything for themselves; but good blokes help each other out.

Liars get tangled up in their own lies; it's honesty that gets blokes out of trouble.

Speaking gently and truthfully will do you good; just like working hard with your hands.

A drongo is always impressed with himself—he suffers from delusions of adequacy! But a bloke who listens to wise advice *is* wise!

A real goose will lose his temper at the drop of a hat; but a smart bloke will hear an insult and just let it go through to the keeper.

A bloke who speaks truth does good; but watch out—there are heaps out there who'll lie and deceive.

Some blokes have got a tongue like a razor blade— it'll cut ya to pieces. But sensible blokes say things that help instead of hurting.

Stick to the gospel truth and you're on solid ground, but start telling porkies and you're gone a million.

A bloke with a sneaky mind is lower than a snake's belly, but a bloke who's straight and above board is gonna be okay.

Lose the booze! *(Proverbs 23:29-35)*

Who's always in hot water? Who's always down in the dumps? Who's always aggro? Who's always whingeing? Who's always in the wars? Who's got bloodshot eyes?

Blokes who spend all day at the pub suckin' down the grog, that's who! They like nothing better than a schooner of the amber fluid, with a rum chaser. With them the grog goes down faster than a bride's nightie, but in the end the stuff bites like a redback!

Before long they're seein' things, and they're as mixed up as a muddle-headed wombat.

They get tossed about like a bloke tryin' to sleep in a cyclone. Then they wake up bashed and bruised all over without a clue what's happened to them. And when they come to, all they can think about is hitting the booze again!

Looking at the big questions *(Proverbs 30:1-9)*

Some wise words from Agur (Jake's son) speaking to his mates.

Sometimes I feel like a complete idiot! I reckon I barely understand enough to draw breath!

I really oughta know more! *Especially* I oughta know God!

But who can get his brain around the greatness of God's heavens? Or grab the wind in his fist? Or get a grip on the oceans? I mean, who but God could have made this vast universe or fabulous planet? If you reckon you know, then tell me his name!

Every word of God is gospel truth! And God is an invisible shield protecting those who rely on him.

God's words are enough—don't try to add to them... otherwise God himself will call you a liar!

Dear God, let me ask two favours from you before I tumble off the twig:

First: keep me superglued to the truth, not lost in lies. Second: stop me from getting dead rich or dead poor—just let me have enough to get by on.

If I'm rich I might say, "Why should I bother with God?" and if I'm poor I might turn to robbery and bring shame on your name.

From John's Gospel

What's the Big Idea? *(John 1:1-18)*

In the beginning there was "The Idea". And it was God's Idea. And there was no real diff between God and God's Idea. Right from the start everything came from this Idea—everything, bar none. This Idea was bursting with life, and it was a really Bright Idea that's never been snuffed out.

God sent a bloke named John to tell us about this Big Idea (which wasn't John's idea, it was God's Idea – John was just a signpost pointing us in the right direction).

God's *Bright Idea* was coming into the world to give everyone the *right idea* (if you catch my drift).

Then he turned up, inside the world *he'd* thought of and *he'd* made. And the world had no idea who he was.

He came to his own mob, and they didn't want to know him.

But those who *did* want to know him he made part of God's own family: not from the natural course of things; or because of their own idea; but because it was all God's idea and God's doing.

Well now, God's Idea became a bloke, and camped here for a bit, and we saw him, and saw just how great he was—the greatness of God's Good Idea, full of good news and generous to a fault.

John swore to us, "This is the bloke I said was coming—my oath he is! He's way ahead of me: the First Idea, long before anything else was ever thought of."

He's all our Christmases rolled into one: just one gift after another! Moses gave us *good advice*, but Jesus Christ gave us *good news*!

No one's ever seen God; but God's Bright Idea (coming from the Father's heart) has given us the right idea about God.

John the Baptist (John 1:19-28)

Now this was John's sworn statement when the head honchos in Jerusalem sent their agents to grill him. They said, "Just who do you think you are?"

John was straight about it, and right up front he said, "I am *not* the Promised One."

So they peppered him with questions: "What then? Do you reckon you're Elijah?"

"Nope."

"Well then, how about... the Prophet?"

"No, no!"

"Come on, help us here. We've gotta take an answer back to the bosses who sent us. So, whadda you say about yourself?"

"I'm just a voice, a messenger, calling out in the bush:

'Open the gate for God!'—just like old Isaiah said."

Members of the PPP (the Pharisees' Pious Party) then asked him, "Well, why are you baptising then? If you're not the Promised One, or Elijah, or the Prophet?"

"Look," said John, "I just baptise with water. But somewhere here among you is the one you don't wanna know. I'm not even good enough to put his thongs on his feet!"

This happened on the Bethany side of the Jordan River, where John was doing his baptising.

He's the one! (John 1:29-34)

The next day John saw Jesus coming towards him, and said: "Look! God's 'Lamb'—who cleans up the mess we make. This is who I meant when I said, 'After me comes the bloke from before me—way before and above me'. I didn't know him, but I came here baptising so that you'd see him when he turned up.'

John explained, "I saw with my own eyes the Spirit fly down like a big white cockatoo out of the heavens, and land on him. Before that happened I didn't know him. But the one who'd sent me to baptise people in the water had said: 'You'll see the Spirit fly down and land on someone. Then you'll know he's the one who'll baptise people in the Spirit.' I'm telling you I've seen this: he's the one! He's God's own Son!"

The first followers (John 1:35-51)

The next day John was there again with a couple of his followers, and he spotted Jesus. John said: "That's him... that's God's 'Lamb'." So his two followers who heard this went over to Jesus.

Looking over his shoulder Jesus saw them coming.

"What are you after?"" he said.

"G'day, sir," they muttered. "Whereabouts are you putting up at the moment?'

"Come and see."

It was already about four o'clock, so they spent the rest of the arvo with him.

One of these two blokes who'd heard John and then gone with Jesus was Simon Peter's brother Andy. He then took off to find Simon, and said to him, "Hey! Guess what? We've found the Promised One!" (The Hebrew word for "Promised One" is *Messiah* and the Greek word is *Christ*.)

Andy brought his brother back to meet Jesus, who said, "So, you're Simon Johnson, eh? I'm giving you the nickname *Cephas*." (In other words—Peter.)

The next day Jesus popped over to Galilee, where he found Phil (from Bethsaida, the same town as Andy and Peter), and said to him, "Follow me." Phil then found Nat, and said, "We've found him! The bloke Moses and the prophets promised. He's Jesus— Joe's son from Nazareth!"

"Nazareth!" Nat said. "You're pulling my leg! Nazareth?"

"Come and see," said Phil. "Just come and see for yourself."

Jesus saw Nat arrive and said, "Here's a fair dinkum Israelite—and an honest bloke."

"How do you know?" Nat asked.

"I saw you under the gumtree before Phil called you."

Nat was gob smacked and said, "Sir, you really *are* God's own Son... it's like being in the presence of royalty!"

"All this just because I said I saw you under the

gumtree?" said Jesus. "You've seen nothing yet. It's dead set certain that you'll see the heavens open, and God's messengers going back and forth between heaven and me: the Promised One."

Wine for the wedding (John 2:1-13)

A few days later there was a big wedding do at Cana (in Galilee Shire) and Jesus and his Mum and his followers were invited.

In the middle of the big do the wine ran out! His Mum, Mary, said to Jesus, "The caterer's run out of wine!"

"What's that gotta do with us, Mother? It really isn't time for me to start yet... "

Mary bustled over to the caterers and said, "Do whatever he tells you."

There were half a dozen big pots there (for the washing ceremony), each holding around a hundred litres. Jesus told the caterers to fill them with water, which they did, right to the brim.

"Now, pour some off into a carafe and take it to the head table," he said.

Which they did, and poured out a glass of the ex-water (which was now wine) for the master of ceremonies (who had no idea where it came from—although the caterers knew). The MC then called the groom to one side and said, "Hey, everyone else serves the best bubbly first, and then, when everyone's a bit sozzled, brings out the cheap stuff, the cask wine. But you've saved the real vintage stuff until now!"

This was the first of the signs Jesus did (in Cana, in Galilee Shire): signs that pointed towards his greatness. And his followers believed and trusted him.

Then Jesus popped down to Capernaum for a few days with his Mum, his brothers, and his followers all in tow.

In the Temple (John 2:14-25)

Just before the big Passover festival Jesus went down to Jerusalem. There he found the plaza around the Inner Temple filled with cattle and sheep for sale, and blokes sitting at a big table with a sign up saying 'Currency Exchange'.

So he tied some cords into a makeshift whip and drove the cattle and sheep out of the Temple, and tipped the money changers' table on its side, sending the coins rolling across the plaza. He said, "Get these things out of here! This is a Temple, not a supermarket!"

His followers remembered the bit from the Bible that says: 'A passion for your house burns in my heart.'

Then the Temple big wigs bowled up and said, "Hey! How can you do this? What right have you got? Come on, show us! What clever sign have got for us?'

Jesus replied, "Rip down this temple and in three days I'll have it together again."

The big wigs sneered, "It took 46 years to build this place! And you reckon you can do it in three days?"

But the 'temple' Jesus meant was his own body, and after he'd come back from the dead his followers remembered what he'd said. Then they believed the words of the Bible and Jesus' words.

During the Passover festival heaps of people believed and trusted Jesus because of the signs they saw him doing. But Jesus didn't trust them—because he could read them like a book. Without being told, Jesus knew them inside out.

A night visitor (John 3:1-21)

Now there was a bloke named Nicodemus who was a city councillor and a member of the PPP (the Pharisees Pious Party). He slipped in to see Jesus at night, and said, "Sir, it's a dead cert that you're a teacher from God—it's clear from all these signs you do. That's just not on unless God's on your side."

Jesus responded: "Now listen! Unless you're born again—from above—you'll never get into God's kingdom."

"Eh?" said Nicodemus. "I don't get it. How can a bloke get born a second time? Come off it! A full grown bloke getting into his mum's womb?"

Jesus explained: "Just listen! Listen carefully. Unless a bloke is born of water and Spirit he can't even get through the front door of God's kingdom. Bodies give birth to bodies—Spirit gives birth to spirit. So don't look so staggered when I tell you that you've gotta be born again—from above. It's a bit like the breeze that blows all over the place. You hear it in the gumtrees but you don't know where any particular puff of wind has come from or where it's going. This 'breeze of the Spirit' that brings a bloke new life from above is a bit like that."

"Well," said Nicodemus, "how can this sort of thing happen?"

Jesus replied: "You reckon you're a teacher of Israel and you don't know? The fact is: I'm telling you what I've seen and know and you don't believe me. If you won't believe what I say about what happens to blokes in *this* world, there's no chance you'll believe what I say about the *next* world. No bloke's ever gone up into heaven—except the bloke who came from there, the Promised One, whose home is heaven. Yonks ago, out in the desert, Moses lifted up an image of a snake. In much the same way, the Promised One must be 'lifted up' so that everyone who believes and trusts him will gain real life, eternal life.

"For God loves the people of this world so much that he's given his one and only Son, so that whoever believes and trusts him won't rot and perish forever, but will live forever. God didn't send his Son to judge, and lock up the people of this world (and throw away the key!) but to rescue them! Whoever believes and trusts him escapes judgement and jail. But unbelievers are judged, and pronounced guilty already, because they refuse to trust God and God's own Son. It's like God struck a match, and they ran off to the dark corners so God wouldn't see what they were up to. Blokes who are up to no good hate the light, and won't come near it—because their ugly thoughts are written all over their faces, and they don't want to be seen. But those who believe the truth gravitate to the light, where they can see that God's behind what they do."

The sheila at the wellhead (John 4:3-42)

Jesus left Judea Shire and headed off to Galilee Shire again. This time he took the Samaria Road, and soon hit the outskirts of the township of Sychar, near the place called Joseph's Paddock (a patch of grazing land Jacob gave his son Joseph). Jacob's old well was still there, and Jesus sat down because he was bushed after the long walk from Jerusalem.

It was lunchtime so his followers popped into town to buy some food. While they were away a Samaritan sheila came to the wellhead with her bucket, and Jesus asked her for a drink of water.

"But you're a Jew!" she said, looking surprised. "And I'm a Samaritan. And a woman! You Jews all look down your long noses at us Samaritans, so how come you've asked me for a schooner of water?"

Jesus answered: "Look—if you'd understood the generosity of God, and who's asking you for a drink now, you'd have turned around and asked me instead, and I'd have given you real, fresh 'living' water."

"Sure! So where's your bucket then? This is a deep well, sunshine, so how are you going to get this 'real, fresh "living" water', eh? Old Jacob dug this well yonks ago, and generations of people, and animals, have been watering here ever since. Do you

reckon you're a bigger wheel than Jacob?"

Jesus explained: "Anyone who drinks from this
well sooner or later gets thirsty again. But my
'water' knocks out thirst forever. It's like having an

artesian bore, bubbling up inside, like a fountain of life forever."

"Well, sir," she said, "I'd like some of that! Then I could give up tramping out here every day for buckets of water!"

Then Jesus told her, "Go home and fetch your husband."

"Haven't got a husband!" she snapped.

"Too right you haven't got a husband!" Jesus said to her. "In fact, up to now you've had five husbands, and the bloke you're living with right now is not yours. So you got that one right!"

"Ah, well now, sir," the woman said, "it turns out that you're a prophet. So, then, answer me this one: where are we supposed to worship? Here on this mountain (like the Samaritans say) or in Jerusalem (like the Jews say)?"

Jesus said to her, "You'd better believe it: the time's coming when it won't be *either* this mountain *or* Jerusalem where you go to worship the Father. You Samaritans don't know who you're worshipping; at least the Jews know, because God's rescue plan comes through the Jews. But the moment is coming (in fact, it's come!) when people all over will worship God the Father for real. God is Spirit, and worshipping him is a whole-of-life, spirit-and-truth thing."

The woman said, "I know the Promised One is coming (the one called the *Christ*), and when he comes he'll explain everything."

"That's me," said Jesus, "the one you're chatting to right now."

Just then his followers bowled up, and thought it was pretty weird that Jesus was talking to a woman (a Samaritan woman!). But none of them was game enough to ask him why.

The woman, meanwhile, had dropped her bucket and run back into town, where she yelled out, "Come and see a bloke who could tell me all about myself—who could see straight through me! Do you reckon he might be the Promised One?" So they all trooped out to see Jesus.

Meanwhile his followers were getting tetchy. "Come on, sir," they said, "eat something."

Jesus said, "I have nourishment you know nothing about."

They were puzzled: "Did someone bring some food while we were gone?"

Jesus explained: "What nourishes me is doing what God wants. Look around—do you reckon it's about four months to the harvest? Well, look again—it's harvest time right now! There are 'paddocks full of people' ready for reaping! Already the harvester's been signed up to get the crop in. The planter and the harvester fill the silos of heaven together, and both are as happy as Larry. God's people have been planting the paddocks for years, and you'll get the crop in—the harvest from their hard work."

Heaps of people from the township of Sychar believed and trusted Jesus because the woman had said, "He told me all about myself—he could see right through me." They came out to the wellhead and asked Jesus to hang around for a couple of days—long enough for lots more to believe and trust him because they'd heard him for themselves.

They said to the woman, "We don't have to take your word for it anymore—now we've heard him ourselves. And you're right, this bloke really is the Promise One!"

The woman caught playing up *(John 8:1-11)*

Early one morning Jesus was down in the Temple plaza, in Jerusalem. He took a seat and started teaching, and the mob crowded around to listen. Then a bunch of lawyers and members of the PPP (Pharisees Pious Party) arrived, dragging a woman who'd been caught in a bloke's bedroom.

They stuck the woman in the middle of the mob, right in front of Jesus, and said, "Sir, this sheila was caught in the act—in the act!—of playing up with a bloke who's not her husband. Now the Old Law of Moses pronounces the death penalty, death by stoning, for this sort of behaviour. But the occupying Roman forces won't let us execute anyone. What do you say?"

(They were just trying to trap Jesus, trying to make him say something they could use against him.)

Jesus acted like he hadn't heard them, bent over and began writing with his finger in the dust. They kept on and on at him, so he stood up and said, "Alright do it—*but* someone who is *perfect* has to throw the first stone." Then he sat down again, and went back to writing in the dust.

Slowly, one by one, they all drifted away (the old

blokes were the first to go!), until Jesus was alone—
with just the woman standing in front of him. Then
he stood up and said, "Well, where are they? Is
there anyone pointing the finger at you now?"

"No one, sir."

"Then I won't point the finger either. Off you go—
but from now on don't do anything to dismay or
disgust God."

The bloke born blind (John 9:1-12)

As he was walking along Jesus saw a bloke who'd
been blind from birth. And his followers asked him,
"Sir, who did the wrong thing that caused this bloke
to be blind? Was it him, or was it his old folks?"

"Neither," said Jesus. "It's not that sort of simple
cause-and-effect thing. But it *is* a chance to show
you the power of God. I've got to get on with
doing God's work while the sunlight lasts, because
there's a darkness coming that will halt the work. In
fact, while I'm here I *am* the sunlight!"

Then he spat on the ground, made a little mud,
and spread some on the man's eyes. "Now," said
Jesus, "go and wash that off in the Dispatch Pool."

The man went to the pool, and washed, and
bingo! He could see!

His mates, and other people who'd seen him
around as a blind man selling pencils said, "Is this
that blind bloke? The one who used to sell pencils?"

"It's him," said some.

"Nah—it can't be," said others. "It just looks like him."

"It's me! It's me!" said the ex-blind-man.

"How on earth did this happen?" they asked.

"A bloke named Jesus made some mud and dabbed it on my eyes and told me to go to the Dispatch Pool and wash, and I did, and suddenly I could see!"

"Well, where's he got to? Where is he now?"

"Actually... I don't know."

The healed man gets grilled (John 9:13-34)

They brought the ex-blind-man to the PPP (the Pharisees Pious Party), because the day when Jesus made the clay and healed the blind bloke was an official Day Off. The Pharisees cross-examined him about what happened.

"He smeared mud on my eyes, I washed it off, and now I can see," was the answer.

Some said, "The bloke who did this is all wrong and ungodly—because he did it on a Day Off." Others said, "But how can an ungodly, wrong-headed bloke pull off a stunt like this?" And they bickered about it.

Then they turned to the ex-blind-man and said, "What can you tell us about this bloke who fixed your eyes?"

"I reckon he's a prophet," he said.

Then the PPP decided it was a fraud, and the man had never been blind in the first place. So they called in his parents and said, "Is this bloke your son? And was he *really* born blind? And how come he can see now?"

"He's definitely our son," they murmured nervously, "and he was definitely blind from birth.

But how come he can see now... well... we haven't got a clue. Ask him. He's a big bloke – he can speak for himself."

They said this because they were afraid of the PPP who'd already promised that anyone who had a good word for Jesus would be kicked out of the Jewish Meeting Hall.

The Pharisees then called the ex-blind-man back in and said, "You oughta thank God you can see again, not this Jesus person—who we happen to know is ungodly and wrong-headed."

"I wouldn't know anything about that. All I know is: I *was* blind and *now* I can see!"

"Tell us again: what did he do? How did he fix your eyes?"

"How many more times? I've told you already. Why do you keep asking? Do you wanna become his followers too?"

They snapped angrily, "*You're* a follower of that man, not *us*! We follow Moses. We know for a fact that God has spoken to us through Moses, but this bloke we've never heard of."

"How very odd! You've never heard of him, but he fixed my eyes. We all know God ignores wicked blokes, but he does things for blokes who serve him. From the dawn of history no one's ever fixed eyes that were completely cactus from birth. If this bloke wasn't on God's side he couldn't have done it either."

"Are you trying to teach grandma how to suck eggs? You're as bad as he is! Sergeant-at-arms—throw this man out!"

A quiet chat *(John 9:35-41)*

When Jesus heard what had happened he tracked down the ex-blind-man and said, "Well now, do you believe in the Promised One?"

"I want to. Who is he?"

"You've seen him," said Jesus, "and he's talking to you right this minute."

"I believe and trust you, sir!" Then he knelt down and said, "Master!"

Jesus said, "I've come into the world to bring everything into focus—so those who've never seen the point will suddenly see, and catch on; and those who reckon they've seen it all will be plunged into darkness."

These words got back to the PPP, who challenged Jesus: "Do you reckon we're blind? Is that what you're saying?"

Jesus said to them, "If you really *were* blind you'd be off the hook. But you claim to see exactly what's going on, so you'll be held accountable."

Lazarus tumbles off the twig *(John 11:1-16)*

In Bethany there was a bloke named Lazarus who was really crook. He was the brother of Martha and Mary – the same Mary who, a bit later, put the aromatherapy oil on Jesus, and wiped his feet with her own hair. She sent a message to Jesus saying, "Master, your good mate is as sick as a dog."

Jesus said, "The end of this won't be death—the end will be praise and thanks to God, and to God's own Son."

Even though Jesus was very fond of the whole family he still hung around for a couple of days where he was before he made a move. Finally he said to his followers, "Let's make tracks back to Judea Shire."

But they said, "Sir, the PPP are after your blood. It's nuts to go back!"

Jesus replied, "Look, we can travel safely in the daylight. When darkness falls, that's when you're likely to be tripped up."

Then he added, "Our old mate Lazarus is punching out a few Zs. I'm going to go and wake him up."

They said, "Well, if he's getting some decent sleep then he must be getting better."

Jesus had been breaking the news to them gently that Lazarus had tumbled off the twig, but they thought he meant he was really having a sleep. So Jesus told them straight, "Lazarus is dead. And I'm glad I wasn't there when he died, because this gives you another chance to believe and trust. Come on, let's make tracks."

Tom (the twin) said, "If you're game, we're game. If you get killed, we'll die with you."

Better than triple by-pass! (John 11:17-44)

When Jesus got there he found Lazarus had been buried four days earlier. Bethany was only about three Ks from Jerusalem, and a bunch of people from there had come with sympathy cards and flowers for Martha and Mary. When word reached Martha that Jesus was coming she dashed out to meet him, leaving Mary in the house.

"Master, if you'd been here," Martha said to Jesus, "he'd still be alive. And even now, I'm certain anything you ask for, God will give you."

Jesus said, "Your brother *will* come back from the dead."

"I'm quite certain," Martha said, "that at the end of history God will bring *everyone* back from the dead—in what's called 'the resurrection'."

Jesus said to her, "I *am* the resurrection—and I am *life*! Anyone who believes me and trusts me will go through death... and come out the other side—alive! Anyone who believes and trusts me will never be caught in the web of death. Martha, do you believe this? Do you trust me?"

"Yes, Master. I personally believe you're the Promised one, God's own Son, on a mission from God."

With these words she nipped off to fetch her sister Mary. Taking her to one side she said, "The Master's here, and he wants to see you." So Mary went straight out to him.

Now Jesus hadn't gone down the main street, but stayed on the outskirts where Martha had met him. When the mob in the house saw Mary duck out so quickly they assumed she was going to the tomb to lay some flowers and have a good cry, so they trooped along after her.

When Mary reached Jesus she knelt down and said, "Master, if you'd been here he'd still be alive."

When Jesus saw her tears, and the tears of the crowd with her, he started to feel angry at all the

heartbreak caused by death and said, "Where's he buried?"

"This way," they said. "Come on, we'll show you."

And there were tears in Jesus' eyes as well.

The crowd from Jerusalem spotted this and said, "He must have been a real mate." But a few of them sneered, "He fixed that blind man's eyes, so why couldn't he have been here to stop his old mate from dying, eh?"

Still feeling deeply disturbed Jesus arrived at the solid rock tomb where Lazarus was buried. "Open the tomb," he ordered.

"It's been four days," said Martha. "It'll really be on the nose by now."

"Remember what I said? Trust me, and you'll see God at work."

So they opened the tomb.

Jesus prayed, "Father, thank you that you always listen to me. I know that you always listen, but I'm saying it now for the sake of these people, so they'll believe and trust, and know you sent me."

Then in a loud voice Jesus ordered, "Lazarus—come here!"

And out he came! The dead man! Still wrapped in his burial shroud, looking like an Egyptian Mummy!

"Unwrap him." said Jesus. "Free him from those bandages."

Murder plot (John 11:45-57)
So, at last, many of the Jerusalem mob, who were with Mary, and saw it happen, believed and trusted Jesus. But some of them scuttled back to the PPP (the Pharisees Pious Party) and blabbed about what Jesus had done.

So the PPP and the head honchos of the Temple called a council meeting and said, "What'll we do now? What he does looks like signs. If we don't put a stop to it now soon *everyone* will believe and trust, and the Roman rulers will get upset and take it out on us for not keeping the crowd under control—and we'll all lose our cushy jobs."

One of them, a bloke named Caiaphas (who held the rotating presidency that year) snapped, "You dopes! It'd be better for this one bloke to die than for everyone to get the chop."

In blurting out this out Caiaphas didn't realise these were prophetic words spoken by him as Temple President—that Jesus would die in place of everyone else... and not just everyone in Jerusalem or Judea Shire, but for God's whole family scattered around the world, bringing them together.

Then they started cooking up their plot to kill Jesus.

Because of this plot, Jesus avoided the crowds. Instead he nicked off to a remote spot called Ephraim, with his followers, and stayed there for a bit.

Soon it was almost Passover festival time again, and heaps of people from all over the shop trekked up to Jerusalem to take part in the festival.

For that reason they had spies hanging around the Temple looking for Jesus. "What do you reckon," they said to each other, "will he come this year? Do you reckon he'll turn up at the Festival?"

The PPP had given orders that if anyone spotted Jesus they should be tipped off at once, so they could grab him.

Back in Bethany (John 12:1-11)
Six days before the big Passover festival Jesus came back to Bethany (home of Lazarus, the ex-dead-man)

where he was guest of honour at a formal dinner. Martha served the food, Lazarus was at the table, and Mary came and knelt down, and put expensive aromatherapy oil on Jesus' feet, and dried them with her own hair. You could smell the oil all through the house.

Then Judas Iscariot (that snake-in-the-grass among the followers) whinged, "That oil's worth a fortune! It ought to have been sold, so we could give the money to the poor." Not that he really cared about the poor: he looked after the petty cash, and he had his hand in the till.

So Jesus said, "Don't give her a hard time. She's prepared my body for its burial. The poor will always be here for you to help, but I won't be around much longer."

When the Jerusalem crowd heard that he was there they trooped out to Bethany, not just to see Jesus but also to see Lazarus, the ex-dead-man. So the head honchos decided they needed to have Lazarus murdered too, because it was on account of him that many believed and trusted Jesus.

Back in Jerusalem (John 12:12-19)

The next day the festival crowd heard that Jesus was on his way to Jerusalem, so they pulled branches off palm trees and charged down the road to meet him, waving their branches and shouting, "Three cheers for the Rescuer... he's on a mission from God... he's the King!"

And Jesus rode along on a young donkey, fulfilling the old prophecy:

Sing, Jerusalem sing!
There's no need to fear a thing,
On a donkey comes your King.

At the time his followers didn't have a clue what was going on, but later, when Jesus had come back from the dead, they remembered and understood that a prophecy had come true right in front of their eyes.

The mob that had seen him call Lazarus out of the tomb were there telling everyone what they'd seen. Because of this mind-blowing sign crowds and crowds of people went after Jesus.

The PPP threw up their hands in disgust and said, "Just look at that! Everyone on earth's charging after him now!"

In the Upper Room *(John 13:1-20)*

It was just before the big Passover Festival. Jesus knew it was time for him to pass on—depart this world and return to his Father. He really loved the loyal group that had hung on with him to the end—and he loved them to the very end!

Judas Iscariot had already given in to that dark devilish idea, planted in his mind, that he should betray Jesus.

Jesus knew that God had put it all in his hands—to come into this world, carry out the big task, and then go back to God. Bearing this in mind, Jesus got up from the table where they were having supper and took off his coat. He picked up the servant's

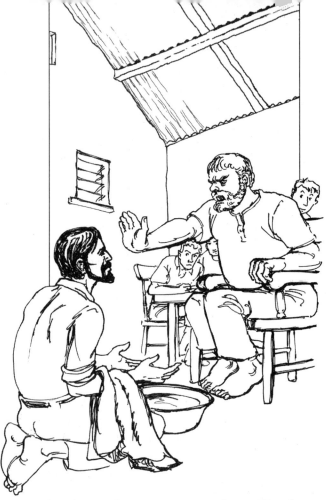

towel, and poured some water into a basin. Then he
began to do the servant's job of washing the feet of
his followers, and wiping them with the towel.

When he got to Peter, Peter spluttered, "But
Master! Washing feet is servants' work! Don't do it!"

Jesus said, "You don't understand just how and

why I'm a servant. But before long you will."

"Stop it!" cried Peter. "Not my feet! Never!"

"Unless I do, you can't be part of all this—one of my people."

"Oh... in that case... don't stop at my feet... keep going... my hands... my face..."

Jesus explained, "Look, this is symbolic. Someone who's had a bath in the morning only needs their feet washed at suppertime. Clean is clean—it works morally and spiritually the same as it works physically. But not for all of you." (Jesus knew who was betraying him, which is why he said, "But not for all of you.")

When he'd finished, put his coat back on, and sat down at the table again, Jesus said, "Do you understand what I've done? You call me "Sir" and "The Master"—which is spot on. Now, if I'm the Master, and I've washed your feet like a servant, then you ought to do the same: serve each other. I've set the pattern, you keep it going! Now listen— a follower's not more important than the bloke he follows. And a messenger's not more important than the bloke who gave him the message. Cotton on to this, and you'll have found the Good Life.

"I'm not including all of you in this. I chose you, and I know you like the back of my hand. And the bit of the Bible has to be fulfilled that says:

> One who sat at the table and shared my bread,
> Now plots and plans to see me dead.

"I'm telling you now, ahead of time, so when it

happens you'll believe and trust me. Now listen to this—whoever welcomes the message about me, welcomes *me*! And whoever welcomes me welcomes The One Who Sent Me."

After this Jesus said, very quietly and seriously, "Listen—one of you will betray me."

At this his followers all shot suspicious looks at each other. Peter whispered to the bloke sitting next to Jesus, "Tell him to tell us who."

So this bloke turned to Jesus and said, "Who? Master, who is it?"

Jesus said quietly, "I'll dip a bit of bread in the gravy and pass it to the bloke who's doing this."

With those words he dipped a bit of bread in the gravy and handed it to Judas Iscariot. When Judas took it utter blackness descended on his heart—the Great Hater took it over. Jesus said, "Go on—do it now."

No one else understood. They thought that because Judas kept the petty cash he was being sent out for food, or to give some money or food to the poor.

With the bit of bread still in his hand, Judas went out into the night.

Once he was gone Jesus said, "Now is the moment when God's greatness is really seen: in his plan for own Son, in the actions of his Son, and in the greatness of what God does for his Son.

"You are beaut mates, and a top team, and I don't have much time left. What I told the crowd I'm telling you—when I take the next step, you can't follow. So here are your marching orders: love each other. I've loved you, now you love each other. This is how they'll know you're my followers: they'll see your love and care for each other."

Peter said, "But what is the next step? Where are you going?"

Jesus said, "Right now you can't come—but later you *will* follow in my steps."

"But why not now?" Peter went on. "I'm ready to die for you if that's what it takes!"

"Really?" Jesus said, "Now listen—before the rooster crows tomorrow morning, *three times* you'll have denied even knowing me!"

Betrayed! *(John 18:1-11)*

Jesus and his followers crossed over Kidron Creek to a spot where there was a garden. Judas (the back stabber) knew this spot because Jesus had often been there with his followers. So Judas got the head honchos to give him a bunch of cops and squadies and followed—armed to the teeth and carrying hurricane lamps.

Jesus knew what was going on, and what was about to happen, so he stepped out to meet them and said, "Who are you looking for?"

They said, "Jesus the Nazarene."

He said, "That's me."

At these words they staggered backwards.

So he said again, "Who are you looking for?"

"For Jesus," they gasped, "the Nazarene."

"I told you—that's me. So if it's me you're looking for, let these other blokes go." This was to fulfil Jesus' prediction that he wouldn't lose even one of those God gave him. Peter whipped out his sword, swung it wildly, and sliced off the ear of Malchus, private secretary to the Council President.

"Put it away, Peter!" said Jesus. "I have to go through with this—I have to drink this cup God's given me."

Jesus alone: charged – and denied (John 18:12-27)

So the cops and the squadies and their commanding officer and the representatives of the head honchos formally arrested Jesus and slipped the handcuffs on him.

First they took him to old Annas, father-in-law of Caiaphas who was Council President at the time. (It was Caiaphas who'd said it would be a great idea for one bloke to die to save everyone else from getting the chop.)

Peter and another member of Jesus' team trailed along behind. This other bloke had a nodding acquaintance with the Council President so he was let into the villa courtyard, while Peter couldn't get past the door. So he went and had a chat to the woman on the door and got Peter in. But this woman said to Peter, "Haven't I see you hanging around with the accused? Aren't you one of his mob?"

"No way!" snapped Peter.

Now the staff of the villa had built a fire in the courtyard, because it was cold, and were gathered around it. Peter joined them, warming his hands at the fire.

Then Annas started giving Jesus the third degree about his followers and his teaching.

Jesus replied, "Everything I've said has been out in the open in plain words. I've spoken in the meeting halls and the temple plaza. There's no secret agenda here. I've been open and straightforward. So why ask me? Ask the crowds that heard me—they'll tell you."

One of the guards beside him thumped Jesus, growling, "Is that how you talk to a former Council President?"

"Tell me what I said that was wrong," said Jesus. "You can't? Then why hit me!"

Then Annas sent Jesus, still handcuffed, on to Caiaphas (the current Council President).

Meanwhile, Peter was in the courtyard, warming himself by the fire. The others said, "Aren't you one of his mob?"

"Nope," said Peter firmly. "Not me!"

Then one of the staff—a relative of the bloke whose ear Peter had lopped off—said, "But didn't I see you in the garden with him?"

Again Peter said no, and at that moment a rooster crowed.

The Governor's judgement (John 18:28-40)

It was still the early hours of the morning when they took Jesus to the Roman governor's castle. The head honchos wouldn't go inside themselves (so they'd still be ritually clean for the big Passover Festival). So Governor Pilate met them at the castle gate and said, "What's the charge against this prisoner?"

They said, "If this bloke wasn't a trouble maker we wouldn't have brought him here."

"Do it yourself," said Pilate. "Put this trouble maker through your own court."

"Ah, but—under your law, we're not allowed to pass the death sentence."

(This fulfilled Jesus' prediction about how he would die.)

Pilate went back inside the castle, summoned Jesus and said, "Well, then, have you been calling yourself 'the King of the Jews'?"

Jesus replied, "Is this your idea? Or are you just parroting those others?"

Pilate said, "Do I look like a Jew? Do I? Your own people brought you here, your own council, so what have you done to upset them?"

Jesus explained, "My kingdom is not political. If it was my followers would be protesting and campaigning against my arrest. But I'm not that sort of king."

"So you *are* a king, then?"

"Those are your words. But this is the truth about why I was born and why I came into this world. Everyone who cares about truth listens to me."

"Huh! What counts as truth!"

With these words the governor went back to the castle gate and said to the head honchos and the crowd, "He doesn't look guilty of anything to me. But I'm supposed to release one prisoner to celebrate your Passover festival. So would you like me to release this 'King of the Jews'?"

"No way," they wailed. "Not this bloke. Never. Instead, give us... Barabbas." (This Barabbas was an armed robber.)

Mocking justice *(John 19:1-16)*

So Pilate ordered Jesus to be whipped. Some of the squadies wove thorns into a mock crown and stuck on his head. And they found an old purple cloak to throw around his shoulders.

"Hey look!" they hooted. "Now he looks like a real King of the Jews!" and they circled around him, punching him.

Governor Pilate went back to the castle gate and said, "Now look—I'm bringing him out again. Get this straight: I reckon he's not guilty." So Jesus came out—wearing the crown of thorns and the old purple robe. And Pilate said, "Look at the prisoner!"

When the head honchos and the Council members saw him they chanted, "Kill him! Kill him!"

"Kill him yourselves!" said Pilate. "I keep telling you—there's no case against this man."

The head honchos replied, "We have a law that says he's gotta die, because he made himself out to be God's own Son."

This made Pilate dead nervous. He went back inside the castle, and said to Jesus, "Where are you from?"

Jesus stayed silent.

"If you won't talk to me I can't help you," said Pilate. "Don't you understand that I can let you go, or I can sign your death warrant?"

Jesus responded, "The only power you have has been given to you—from above. The bloke who betrayed me is more guilty."

At these words Governor Pilate tried again to release Jesus. But the head honchos said, "Only an enemy of the Emperor would let this man go! Anyone who claims to be a 'king' is a rebel against the Empire."

At this Pilate brought Jesus out to his official magistrate's dais in the castle courtyard (the Hebrew word is *Gabbatha* or 'The Pavement'). By now it was about midday (of the day before Passover), and Pilate announced: "Look—your king!"

"Take him! Kill him!" they shouted. "Take him! Kill him!"

"Kill your king? Are you serious?"

"We have no king," said the Council members, "just the Emperor."

Then Pilate signed the death warrant.

Skull Rock *(John 19:17-27)*

They led Jesus out, carrying his own heavy wooden scaffold, to the place called 'Skull Rock'. There they nailed him to a cross. There were two others killed that day—one on either side of him, and Jesus in the middle.

Governor Pilate had a sign put on his cross reading: "Jesus the Nazarene, the King of the Jews."

A huge crowd read this sign because the execution site was near the city, and the sign was in Hebrew, Latin and Greek. So the Council went back to Pilate and complained, "Don't write 'The King of the Jews', but 'He *said* he was King of the Jews'!" Pilate said, "What I've written, stays put!"

The four man execution squad divided Jesus' clothes up equally, one share each. But his robe was a single woven piece of fabric. So they said, "Let's

not tear this into four parts and ruin it, but roll the dice and the winner gets the whole thing." This fulfilled something the Bible said:

> "They shared out my clothes,
> And rolled dice for my robe."

And so that's what the squad did.

Close by stood Jesus' mother, his Aunt Mary (wife of Clopas) and Mary Magdalene. When Jesus saw his

mother, and standing nearby the team member who
was his best mate, he said, "Mother... he'll be a son
to you." And to his mate he said, "Look after her...
like a mother." (From then on that bloke looked
after Mary, and gave her a home.)

Jesus dies (John 19:28-37)

Jesus knew then that everything was done. To fulfil
a bit of the Bible he said, "I'm thirsty." A bottle of
sour wine was there, so a sponge soaked with it
was lifted up, on the end of a spear, to his mouth.

He had a taste, and then said, "It's all over...
completed... finished!"

Then Jesus bowed his head—and gave up his spirit.

Because it was the day before the Passover festival
the Council didn't want the bodies to remain on
their crosses overnight. They asked Governor Pilate
to order their legs to be broken, so they'd die
quickly and could be taken down. So the squad
broke the legs of the criminals on either side of
Jesus, but when they came to him they didn't
bother because he was already dead. To make sure,
one soldier stuck his spear in Jesus' side, and blood
and water came out. (You're getting an eyewitness
testimony at this point—a truthful eyewitness
testimony.)

These events fulfilled those bits of the Bible that
said:

> "Not a bone was broken" and
> "They'll see the one they pierced".

Jesus is buried *(John 19:38-42)*

Now Joseph of Arimathea (a secret follower of Jesus, because he was afraid of the Council) asked Governor Pilate for the body. When Pilate said okay he came and took the corpse, with the help of the man who'd visited Jesus after dark, Nicodemus—who brought a heap of embalming ointment, made from myrrh and aloes.

Following the usual burial practice they wrapped up Jesus' corpse in a shroud together with the ointment.

Not far from the execution site was a garden, and in the garden a brand new rock tomb. That's where they buried Jesus, because they had to hurry and get it done before sunset (and the start of Passover).

Jesus is alive! *(John 20:1-10)*

On Sunday morning, before sunrise, Mary Magdalene set off for the tomb. She found the heavy stone that had sealed the entrance rolled away.

At this she took off like a rabbit and ran back to where the team was staying. She found Peter, and that other team member who was a good mate of Jesus, and puffed out, "He's gone! Someone's taken him! And I don't know where!"

Peter and the other bloke took off for the tomb at top speed. The other bloke got there first and looked inside. Sure enough, apart from the burial sheet the tomb was empty. Then Peter caught up, went inside, and saw the empty tomb, and the burial sheet, with the cloth that had been wound around the head of the corpse lying separately.

The other bloke came in after Peter, saw all of this, and he was the first one to believe what had happened—even though, at the time they didn't understand that the Bible said that Jesus would come back from the dead.

Mary sees Jesus (John 20:11-18)

Mary was standing in the garden, outside the tomb, crying her eyes out. Still crying, she stooped down and looked inside. She saw two angels in white, one sitting where the head would have been and the other where the feet would have been.

"Now then," they said, "why all these tears?"

"They've taken him," she sobbed. "The Master's been taken. And I don't know where."

As she said this she turned back to the garden and saw Jesus standing there, without knowing it was Jesus.

"Now then," he said to her, "why all these tears? Who are you looking for?"

Taking him for the gardener she sobbed, "Oh, please, if you took him, just tell me where—and I'll come and fetch him."

Jesus said to her, "Mary!"

She turned to face him and cried out, "Teacher!"

He said, "Now, now, don't cling to me like that. I've got to go. I've got to go to the Father. But you whiz back to the team and tell them that I'm going to my Father and your Father, to my God and your God."

Mary rushed back and told the others that she'd seen the Master. And she told them what he'd said.

Others see Jesus (John 20:19-23)

That same day (a Sunday) at sunset, when the team was in hiding in the house with all the doors shut (because they were still afraid of the Temple authorities) Jesus came.

He stood in the middle of the room, greeted them with the word, "Peace!" and then showed them the wounds in his hands and in his side.

They were beside themselves with excitement and happiness to see the Master.

Again Jesus said, "Peace be with you!" adding, "Just as the Father sent me, so I'm sending you." Taking a deep breath he said, "Receive my Spirit. If you forgive someone's wrongdoings they're forgiven. If you don't, they aren't."

Thomas sees Jesus *(John 20:24-29)*

Although Thomas (who was a twin) was one of the team he wasn't with them that night. So when the others said, "Hey! We've seen the Lord!" Tom said, "Pull the other leg! Unless I see the nail wounds in his hands—and *touch them*—and the wound in his side too—I just won't believe it!"

Eight days later they were together again, and Tom was with them this time. And even though the doors were shut, Jesus came and stood in the middle of the room and greeted them.

Then Jesus said to Thomas, "Come on—reach out your hand and touch these wounds—in my hands and my side. Give up your niggling doubts, and trust me!"

Thomas was gob smacked and said, "You are my Lord—and my God!"

Jesus said, "You trust me because you've seen me. But really well off are those who haven't seen me, but trust me just the same."

The purpose *(John 20:30-31)*

All of this has been written down so that you can trust Jesus as the Promised One, the Christ, God's own Son. And so that—by trusting him, personally

—you can have real life (with God, starting here and now, and going on... forever!).

His mates see Jesus (John 21:1-14)

A bit later Jesus' mates saw him on the shore of Lake Tiberias. It was like this.

There was a bunch of them there: Peter, Tom, Nathan, the two Zebedee boys, and a couple of others.

Peter said, "I'm going to do a spot of fishing."

"Good idea," said the others, "we'll come too."

So they went out in the boat, fished all night, and didn't even catch a tiddler.

About sunrise the next morning Jesus stood on the shore (but they didn't recognise him). He called out, "Caught anything?"

"Nope, not a thing" they shouted.

So he called out, "Drop your net over the right side of the boat—try again."

They did what he said, and this time the net was so full they couldn't pull the thing back into the boat. John said to Peter, "Hey! It's the Lord!"

When Peter heard it was the Lord he grabbed the coat he'd taken off (when he was working), jumped into the water, and headed for shore. The others stayed in the boat (about 100 metres out) and, dragging the full net behind them, rowed back in.

When they landed they found a campfire going and fish and bread already cooking. Jesus said, "Fetch some of the fish you've just caught."

It was Peter who dragged the net up on to the beach. They counted the fish: 153 whoppers! And the net didn't rip!

"Come on," said Jesus, "breakfast's on." None of them was game enough to say, "Who are you?" because they were sure it was him.

Jesus shared out the fresh bread and the barbecued fish. This was the third time they'd seen him since he'd come back from the dead.

Jesus and Peter *(John 21:15-19)*

After breakfast Jesus turned to Peter and asked, "Peter Johnson—do you love me more than these others do?"

Peter said, "You bet! I'm your mate alright!"

"Then feed my lambs."

A second time Jesus said, "Peter Johnson—do you love me more than these others do?"

Peter said, "Yes, Master—you know I'm your mate."

"Then look after my sheep."

A third time Jesus said, "Peter Johnson—do you love me more than these others do?"

Peter was really cut because he'd been asked this question three times. He replied, "Master, you know everything—so you know I love you."

"Then feed my sheep," Jesus said. Then he added, "when you were young you dressed yourself and went wherever you wanted. When you're old you'll hold out your arms, others will dress you, and they'll take you where you don't want to go." Jesus said this to let Peter know what kind of death he would die, and that his death would point people to God.

Finally Jesus said to Peter, "Follow me!"

Jesus and John *(John 21:20-24)*

Peter turned around and saw John, the team member who'd always been a real mate to Jesus, walking behind them. It was John who'd sat next to Jesus at their last meal before his death, and said, "Lord, who is the traitor?"

Peter saw John and said, "What about this bloke, Lord—what'll happen to him?"

Jesus said, "That's not your concern. If I want him to live until I come back, what concern is that of yours? Your job is to follow me!"

That's why some people at the time went around saying that John wouldn't die. But Jesus didn't say that John wouldn't die. He just said, "*If* I want him to live..."

John is the eyewitness to these things—and he's known to be a truthful bloke.

The last word *(John 21:25)*

There are heaps of other things that Jesus did, and if all of them were written down, the whole planet would be drowning in books about Jesus!

From John's first letter

An email from John *(1:1-10)*

G'day!

Well, we saw with our own eyes, and heard with
our own ears, (and even touched with our hands!)
the Beginner—The One who kick started the
universe into life: God's Living Idea. Right in front
of our eyes was the eternal life of God. And we're
just telling you what we saw and heard—so that
you can join the family too—the team run by the
Father and the Son: Jesus the Promised One.

Passing on this terrific news is what we reckon
is fun.

This is *his* message that we're passing on: that God's
character is all sunlight—openness and understanding—
without a single shadow. If I said I was on God's
team but was still slinking around in the shadows,
I'd just be lying. But if we live in openness and
understanding, reflecting the sunlight of God's
character, then we really *are* on the team, and the
death of Jesus washes away all our wrongdoing.

If we say we don't do anything wrong then we're

just hiding things and fooling ourselves and wouldn't know the truth if it bit us on the ankle. But if we admit our wrongdoing (the mess we've made) he's trustworthy, reliable, dependable and will forgive us and pardon us and wash us clean. On the other hand, if we say we're fine (no stains, no shadows) then we're flat out liars and haven't got a clue about God.

Being fair dinkum *(2:1-6)*

My little mates, I'm rabbiting on like this so that you won't go wrong. But if someone *does* lose the plot and wander off the track, we've got someone who'll stick up for us with the Father—Jesus Christ, who *always* got it right! He's taken the hiding we deserve, and paid our debt to God—and not only ours, but everyone's.

And here's how we can be dead sure we're his mate and onside with him—by doing what he says! Anyone who reckons he's okay with Jesus, but *doesn't* follow his instructions is a dead set liar—they think *The Truth* is a newspaper, and they couldn't lie straight in bed! But those who do what they're told, learn from the doing and learn to really and truly love God. This is being fair dinkum: following in the footsteps of Jesus, and becoming more like him.

Getting it right *(2:7-17)*

These are not new orders, old mate—they're the same old orders we had from the off. But I reckon in a sense it *is* new, because it's like sunrise—and now we can start to see the landscape, and see why the old map, the old orders, made sense. Anyone who reckons he's part of the new dawn, but is a "good hater"... well, his brain is blindfolded, and it's still midnight in his mind. He's stumbling around in the dark, without a clue where he's going.

Look, I'm rabbiting on like this, my little mates, because Jesus has forgiven you for ignoring God and, as a result, stuffing things up.

And you old blokes, I'm going on to you like this because you know Jesus, who was in the first chapter of this whole yarn. And I'm going on about it to you young blokes because you give the devil hell; and to you little nippers because you know God as your Father; and to you blokes who are dads, because you know Jesus who wrote the first chapter and is still telling this yarn; and to you young blokes because you're as tough as ironbark, and you're full of God's message, and you're going on giving the devil hell!

Don't get sucked in by the world's ways. If you buy the lies of the world, then your heart's *not* in the right place, and you don't really and truly love God. The world treasures rubbish—it calls sex "love" and pride "self esteem". And the world won't last (the bird you're lusting after now will be old and wrinkly one day, and so will you!)—but the bloke who follows God's orders is home, safe, forever.

Thinking straight (2:18-29)

This is what we call "five-minutes-to-Midnight" time. You've heard that the Enemy of Jesus is on the prowl—and enemies of Jesus are already coming out of the woodwork—which is how we know it's "five-minutes-to-Midnight" time. Some of them reckon they were (or are) Christians—but they never really were, or they wouldn't be attacking now. When they turned nasty that proved they never really belonged to Jesus or his team.

But God's put his hand on you and turned on the light bulb in your brain so you can see the truth. I've dropped you this line not because you don't already know the truth, but so that you'll pick the lies that try to look like the truth.

And who is the liar? Whoever says Jesus is not the Promised One. That's the enemy—the bloke who denies God the Father and Jesus the Son. Whoever denies Jesus, denies God! But whoever serves Jesus, serves God. So hang on to what you learned at the start. If you're firmly planted in that truth, then Jesus and God are firmly planted in you. And what that delivers is eternal life (forever in the Father's family)!

This note is a bit of a warning about those who want to suck you in to the rubbish around you. But God's light can't be turned off. It's like a lighthouse that keeps you off the rocks and on course, so you don't need me to tell you. You know it's fair dinkum, and not a load of old rope, so stick to it.

And, my little mates, stick to Jesus—so that when you're face to face with him you won't suddenly feel all stupid and be looking down at your boots, and shuffling your feet. You know that he's dead straight, and so's everyone who follows in his tracks.

Following orders (3:1-10)

Just take a long, hard squiz at this: God—God *himself* —loves us so much he's adopted us into his family! We're his kids! Of course, the world can't see this, because the world shuts its eyes to God. Yes, we're already in the family and on the team—we've got with the strength. And that's just the start. So, who knows how we'll end up?

In fact, when he turns up, it'll turn out that we have a family resemblance to the Father—and we'll see him the way he really truly is. And everyone who's nailed his hopes to God's promises will try to keep himself clean—because God's perfectly clean.

Anyone who does the wrong thing is a wrongdoer—someone who ignores God. Jesus was able to come and clean up wrongdoing because he never ignored God. No one who is part and parcel of Jesus can wallow in the muck and enjoy doing wrong. Choosing grubby wrongdoing is advertising that you haven't a clue about Jesus.

My little mates, don't let anyone steer you crooked on this. Anyone who lives in the world's wide way has gone to the devil (because the devil ignored God from the start). Jesus came to earth to liquidate the devil's assets, and cancel all the devil's cheques.

No one who loves God ignores God. God's hand is on him and he *can't* ignore God *because* he loves God. This is how you can pick 'em: God's team and the devil's team—whoever ignores God doesn't love God (and doesn't really and truly love anyone else either)!

Love is not just a word *(3:11-24)*

This is the message that we heard from the off: that we ought to love each other—and not be like Cain who ended up killing his own brother. And for why? Because his brother's goodness made him feel rotten—that's why! *Of course* the world can't stand the sight of you!

We know we've made the big shift from the dead world into God's life because we love each other. Any bloke who doesn't really love is as dead as a doornail. Hating is the same as killing! And no one who has murder in his heart is part of God's forever family.

Here's how we know what love really is: Jesus put his life on the line for us. And we ought to put our life on the line for others. But if anyone has a few quid, and he sees someone else who's scratching, and won't help, that shows that he hasn't got a clue about God's love. My little mates, don't just rabbit on about love—*do it.*

This is how we can be dead sure we're onside with God and part of his team. If *this* is how we live, then we don't need to feel guilty. Trust God, not your feelings!

God will give you the big tick—and look after your needs—because you're following his orders. And these are his marching orders: that we trust Jesus and love each other. Those people who follow God's orders are part and parcel of God and he's part and parcel of them. We know this because we've got his Spirit.

Faith at work *(4:1-6)*

My good mates, don't believe everything you hear, but check everything out against God's Book. The world is full of cunning fakers and self-deluded dills. Here's the test: a message that focuses on the Bible's message (that Jesus, the Promised One, has come into this world) is God's message. And every message that shoots off in some other direction is an enemy message. You heard that the enemy was coming—well, the attacks have already begun!

But, my little mates, you've already survived the attacks because your foundation is God, and God is miles greater than the enemy. They belong to this world, and what they say suits this world, so for them the world's all ears.

But we're firmly planted in God. Those who are part of God's family will want to listen, but those who aren't will shut their ears. *Who listens* gives you a clue to which are the true messages and which are the "mistaken" messages!

Heart of love *(4:7-21)*

My good mates—keep going! Keep on being thoughtful and loving to each other because love is the language of God. If we're *able* to be thoughtful and loving that shows that God's been at work in us.

Anyone who can't do "thoughtful and loving" hasn't a clue about God, because God is the heart of love. God actually showed us what "love" really means by sending his own son, Jesus, on his fatal rescue mission into this world, so that we'd end up alive not dead.

What's *real* love? It's not us loving God, it's God loving us, and sending his own son to take the death penalty our wrongdoing deserved. If God loves us like that, then we shouldn't hold back, but do "thoughtful and loving" for each other—no matter what the cost!

No one has ever actually eyeballed God, but when we're being thoughtful and loving to each other that's the evidence that God's at work in us, growing us. In fact, it's how we know we're part and parcel of him, and he's part and parcel of us— it's the share in his own Spirit he's given us.

And we have seen, and can swear on oath, that the Father has sent his own son to be the Rescuer and Ruler of the world. It really happened! Any bloke who's prepared to stand up and say that Jesus is God's own son, well, God's firmly planted in him, and he's firmly planted in God.

So, we know and trust that love is the plan God has for us. And the bloke who's thoughtful and loving is living out the plan, with God's help. This is what being grown up means: being confident that in the High Court of Heaven we won't feel stupid or embarrassed because we've been part of the plan— the loving, thoughtful plan.

We don't need to be frightened of the terrifying power of God, because God's love banishes fear the way turning on the light banishes the shadows, and anyone who's still afraid just hasn't really grown up yet.

Any bloke who says, "I love God" and is still a "good hater" is a flat out liar. If you can't love the people you've seen, how on earth are you going to love the God you haven't seen? Remember: these are our marching orders—if we love God, we have to love each other too.

Aim for the goal (5:1-5)

If you believe and trust that Jesus really is the Promised One, God's own son, then you're a member of God's family. And whoever loves the Father loves the rest of the family as well! And here's how it shows up: we love by obeying his orders. That's what "loving God" actually means—it means following orders. And his orders are never a hard ask.

Whatever God starts, God finishes—and the world can't get in the way! What wins over the world is—our faith (our trust, reliance, dependence on God). Who wins over the world? The bloke who's confident that Jesus is God's own son!

The one and only (5:6-12)

When Jesus was executed we saw blood and water come out of his body—*both* blood and water, mind! Water—because he was baptised to identify with us; blood—because that's the evidence of death, and he died for us. And the third witness who backs this up is the Spirit, the Messenger, who points us towards Jesus.

If a court's prepared to believe evidence given by people, evidence given by God has got to be miles better—and God takes the stand to give evidence for his own son, Jesus.

Any bloke who believes and trusts Jesus has this evidence *inside*. But the bloke who doesn't believe and trust Jesus is calling God a liar!

When God takes the stand to give evidence, what

does he say? He says, "Here's the gift of eternal life, through my own son, Jesus." In other words, this sort of life comes from being part and parcel with Jesus (while those who ignore Jesus, miss out).

Certainties *(5:13-21)*

I've dropped you these few lines so that you'll trust and believe Jesus (God's own son) and, in that way, be locked in to eternal life. We're confident he listens to us, and gives us what's best for us. (We can talk to him about anything, confident that he'll take on our concerns, and provide for us.)

Suppose you see a mate doing the wrong thing—not something fatal, but the wrong thing. Pray about it, and that bloke will be pulled back from the precipice, back into eternal life. All wrongdoing involves turning away from God— but not all wrongdoing is turning away from God *forever*.

A bloke who's been adopted by God into the forever family won't keep plunging back and back into stuff that dismays and disgusts God (the devil just can't get a firm grip on him)!

We just *know* that we're on God's team, and that the world is on the other side, under the Enemy.

We know that Jesus, God's own son, has come and shown us what God's really and truly like. And because of Jesus we now belong to God, and have life with God—starting here and now, and going on forever.

My little mates, keep away from the obsessions of the world around you.

All the best,

Your old mate,

John

Glossary

A
amber fluid – beer
ankle biters – children
ankle, to – to walk
arvo – afternoon
as mad as a cut snake – angry

B
beauty/beaut – good (a word of general approval)
bewdy – good (a word of general approval: the way Aussies often pronounce "beauty")
billy – short for 'billy can' (container for boiling water on a campfire to make tea)
bloke – man or boy
boss cocky – the one in charge
bottler – good (a word of general approval: it comes from the expression "Your blood's worth bottling!")
brass razoo – a fictional coin: "not a brass razoo" means having no money

bright as a box of budgies – really bright, and lively and full of interest

budgie – small bird

bush telegraph – the grape vine (general gossip or news)

bushed – tired, weary

bushrangers – thieves operating on the open road

C

cark – die

chockers – full ('chock full')

chuck – throw

chuck a wobbly – panic

codger – old person

completely cactus – broken, not working

cotton on – understand

couldn't lie straight in bed – habitual liar

crack a keg – turn on the beer

cronies – friends, collaborators

crook – sick

D

damper – bread

dill – someone who's not real bright, a bit slow on the uptake

dough – money

drongo – a foolish person

drover – rural worker, shifting animals from one place to another

E

earbash – talk, lecture ('given an earbashing' means spoken to, or lectured)

F

fair dinkum – genuine, reliable

G

g'day – greeting ('good day')

get a grip – pull yourself together

gibber desert – stony desert

giving heaps – giving trouble, being aggressive

going bananas – excited

goner – dead or destroyed

good onya – an expression of encouragement; the odd way Aussies say "Good on you!"

goose – a foolish person

grub – food

H

happy as Larry – happy

head honchos – people in power

hiding – punishment

homestead – ranch house; home

hunky dory – all right, okay

K

Ks – kilometres

L

long paddock, the – the grass that grows beside the roads and stock routes

M

mallee scrub – shrubbery
mate – friend
merino – sheep
mob – crowd
mug – fool
mulga – the bush, or countryside

N

nag – horse
noggin – head
nope – no
no worries – an expression of agreement

O

old man – a father
Old Nick – Satan
onya – expression of support and approval (short for 'good on you')

P

paddock – field
porkies – lies (rhyming slang: "pork pies")
punching out a few Zs – sleeping

R

rabbiting on – talking

redback – a poisonous Australian spider (a type of black widow)

rellies (or rels) – relatives

ridgy didge – genuine, real

rip into it – get started

rip off merchant – con man, cheat

S

saltbush plain – semi desert country; very flat and sparsely vegetated

sheila – woman or girl

spot on – correct

squaddies – soldiers

squiz – look

stack on a turn – become angry

starve the lizards – expression of surprise

stockman – rural worker show looks after sheep, cattle, goats etc.

stone the crows – expression of surprise

stunned mullet – the look of someone who has been surprised

swag – the backpack carried by itinerant workers

swaggie – short for "swagman"; back in the old days swaggies would tramp "down the wallaby track" from station to station looking for work (or, more likely, for a hand-out and a free feed!)

T

taipan – a type of highly poisonous snake
teed off – annoyed
thick as three short planks – stupid
tick off – lecture, tell off, reprimand
tickled pink – pleased
tinnie – a can of beer
toddler – small child
toffee nose – snob, self important person
tumble off the twig – die

W

wallaby track – the roads tramped down by
   itinerant workers
whinge – complain
whiz – quickly
wowser – one who objects to low morals
wrinkly – old

Y

yarn – story
yonks – years (usually in the sense of 'many years')

Z

z's/a few z's – sleeping. is "punching out a few Zs"

Get your fair dinkum copy of the original for just five bucks!

The Good News Australia New Testament tells all about Jesus and the beginnings of the church and is translated from the original Greek texts written about 2000 years ago. It's been put into contemporary English, and it is a great read.

This booklet and its companion volume, *The Aussie Bible (Well bits of it anyway!)* only tell some of the wonderful story. Be the full bottle on this Jesus bloke and get your own copy of the *Good News Australia New Testament.* You can do this by taking this tear-out coupon/ page to our bookshops or mailing together with your payment of $5 (+$3 postage & handling) to any of the addresses given below.

If you can't get into a Bible Society bookshop or office, ring us on **1 300 139 179** or visit **www.theaussiebible.com.au**

Bible Society bookshops and offices:

NSW
213 Clarence St,
Sydney NSW 2000
(02) 9262 6355

SA
133 Rundle Mall,
Adelaide SA 5000
(08) 8223 3833

NT
Locked Bag 3,
Minto NSW 2566

VIC
212 Main Street,
Lilydale VIC 3140
(03) 9877 9277

WA
Locked Bag 3,
Minto NSW 2566

QLD
Locked Bag 3,
Minto NSW 2566

TAS
Locked Bag 3,
Minto NSW 2566

Good News Australia New Testaments are $8 each by mail. This offer applies to residents in Australia — offer expires 31st December 2007.

The Bible Society in Australia
30 York Road, Ingleburn
2565 NSW Australia
1 300 139 179